Steve

Contents:

Introduction:

Welcome to the exciting world of cricket, where legends are born and heroes are made! In the pages that follow, we will embark on a thrilling journey through the life and career of one of cricket's brightest stars, Steve Smith. This book is part of our Cricket Heroes series, specially crafted for curious minds aged 7 to 12, who are eager to discover the captivating stories of their sporting idols.

Steve Smith's tale is one of dedication, passion, and the unwavering pursuit of excellence on the cricket pitch. From a young boy with a dream in Sydney, Australia, to becoming one of the most renowned cricketers on the planet, Smith's journey is nothing short of extraordinary.

Steve Smith

As we turn the pages, you will witness Smith's rise from a cricket-loving kid to a dynamic leader who led the Australian cricket team to numerous victories. Along the way, we'll explore his remarkable batting prowess, his unique techniques, and the unforgettable moments that have made him a household name in the cricketing world.

But this story is not just about cricket; it's about determination, resilience, and the importance of never giving up on your dreams. So, grab your cricket bat, put on your favourite jersey, and join us as we delve into the life and career of Steve Smith

Chapter 1: A Cricket Dream Begins

In the quiet suburb of Sydney, Australia, nestled amidst tree-lined streets and friendly neighbours, there lived a young boy named Steve Smith. From the very moment he could hold a cricket bat, he was entranced by the sport. His eyes would light up at the mere mention of cricket, and his days were filled with dreams of hitting boundaries and taking wickets.

As a child, Steve was an avid observer of the game. He would sit in front of the television for hours, watching cricket matches from around the world, absorbing the artistry of the players and learning the strategies of the game. But he didn't just watch; he practiced endlessly in the backyard, perfecting his shots and perfecting his bowling action. His parents often marvelled at his dedication and knew that there was something special about their son's passion for cricket.

It wasn't long before Steve's parents, Peter and Gillian, recognized his extraordinary talent. They saw the way his eyes sparkled when he held a cricket ball, and they saw the determination in his young heart. They decided to support his cricket dream wholeheartedly. Peter became his first coach, and Gillian, his biggest cheerleader.

Every weekend, they would take him to the local cricket club, where Steve would eagerly don his cricket whites and step onto the field. He was the youngest on the team, but his skills were far beyond his years. Whether he was facing a fast bowler or sending the ball sailing over the boundary, it was evident that young Steve was a cricket prodigy in the making.

As the sun dipped below the horizon, casting a golden hue across the cricket field, Steve would stay back after practice, honing his skills until darkness shrouded the pitch. His unwavering dedication and the glimmer of ambition in his eyes set him apart from the other kids at the club. He wasn't just playing cricket; he was living his dream.

In those early years, the dream was simple: to play for the Australian national cricket team, to wear the iconic Baggy Green cap, and to hear the roar of the crowd as he stepped onto the hallowed grounds of cricket stadiums around the world. Little did Steve know that this dream was the beginning of an incredible journey that would take him from the local cricket club to the pinnacle of international cricket.

As we turn the pages of this book, we will follow Steve Smith on his remarkable journey, filled with challenges, triumphs, and the unwavering pursuit of excellence in the game he loved so dearly. This is the story of a young boy with a cricket dream, a dream that would soon become a reality and inspire cricket fans worldwide.

Chapter 2: The Journey to the Big League

Steve Smith's cricket journey was marked by dedication, countless hours of practice, and an unshakeable belief in his abilities. As he grew older, his passion for the sport only intensified, and he began to set his sights on bigger goals.

At the age of 10, Steve made a significant move that would shape his cricketing future. His family decided to relocate to Sydney's Sutherland Shire, a region known for producing cricket talent. This move wasn't just about changing addresses; it was about giving young Steve access to better coaching and more competitive cricket. It was a decision that would prove pivotal in his development as a cricketer.

In the Sutherland Shire, Steve joined the Sutherland District Cricket Club, a renowned institution with a rich history of nurturing young talent. Here, he found himself surrounded by like-minded individuals who shared his passion for the game. The club became his second home, and the cricket field, his playground.

Under the guidance of experienced coaches and mentors, Steve's skills blossomed. He fine-tuned his batting technique, worked tirelessly on his bowling action, and developed a deep understanding of the game's nuances. His performances in junior matches caught the eye of selectors, and soon, he was representing Sutherland District at various age levels.

Steve Smith

One of the most significant moments in Steve's early cricketing journey came when he was selected to play for New South Wales at the Under-17 level. It was a proud moment for him and his family, as he wore the state colours for the first time. Steve's performances in state-level competitions were consistently impressive, and he rapidly progressed through the ranks.

But it wasn't all smooth sailing. Steve faced challenges and setbacks along the way. There were matches when he struggled to find his form, moments when he questioned whether he was on the right path. However, it was during these testing times that he displayed a quality that would define his career—resilience. Steve refused to be disheartened by temporary setbacks; instead, he used them as stepping stones to improvement.

Steve Smith

As he entered his teenage years, Steve Smith's name began to resonate beyond the boundaries of local cricket grounds. Cricket enthusiasts across Australia started to take notice of this young, talented all-rounder who seemed destined for greatness. The dream of playing for the Australian national team was no longer a distant fantasy; it was a goal that was becoming more achievable with each passing day.

In the next chapter, we will delve into Steve's journey through the junior ranks of Australian cricket and the momentous milestones that brought him closer to his dream of donning the Baggy Green cap.

Chapter 3: Joining the Ranks of Baggy Green

The sun was shining brightly over the hallowed Sydney Cricket Ground (SCG) on a warm summer's day. The year was 2010, and the Australian cricket team was preparing to face Pakistan in a Test match. It was an ordinary day for most, but for a young Steve Smith, it marked the beginning of an extraordinary journey.

Steve had been called up to join the Australian national cricket team for the very first time. The dream he had nurtured since childhood was now tantalizingly close to becoming a reality. He couldn't believe that he was about to wear the coveted Baggy Green cap, an emblem of honour and a symbol of excellence in the world of cricket.

As he entered the dressing room, Steve's heart raced. He saw the names of cricket legends like Ricky Ponting, Shane Watson, and Michael Clarke on the jerseys hanging beside his. It was an awe-inspiring moment for the 21-year-old, who had watched these players on TV just a few years ago.

The match against Pakistan was a turning point in Steve's career. Though he was initially selected as a leg-spinning all-rounder, his batting prowess quickly came to the forefront. In his debut Test, he played a crucial innings, scoring 77 runs. It was a glimpse of the batting brilliance that would soon become his trademark.

But it wasn't just Steve's batting that stood out; it was his unbridled enthusiasm on the field. He was known for his spectacular catches, his sharp reflexes in the slip cordon, and his ability to turn the game with both bat and ball. He was a true all-rounder in every sense.

As Test match after Test match passed, Steve's performances continued to impress. His batting averages climbed steadily, and he was soon recognized as one of the most promising young talents in world cricket. He became known for his unorthodox but highly effective batting style, which included a unique technique that involved shuffling across the crease.

In 2013, Steve was appointed as the captain of the Australian cricket team, a role that would define his career in more ways than one. As captain, he was not only responsible for his individual performance but also for leading the team to victory. His leadership style was characterized by passion, determination, and an unwavering commitment to the Baggy Green.

Under Steve Smith's leadership, the Australian team achieved remarkable success, including regaining the Ashes urn from England and reaching the number one ranking in Test cricket. He led by example, always willing to put in the hard yards and inspire his teammates with his dedication to the game.

Steve Smith's journey from a young cricket enthusiast to the captain of the Australian national cricket team was nothing short of remarkable. In the next chapter, we will delve deeper into the challenges and triumphs of his captaincy and the pivotal moments that shaped his career.

Chapter 4: The Rise of a Batting Genius

As Steve Smith's career blossomed, so did his reputation as a batting genius. His unorthodox but highly effective technique, characterized by his unique shuffle across the crease, became a subject of intrigue and admiration among cricket enthusiasts worldwide. In this chapter, we explore the evolution of Steve Smith's batting prowess and some of his most memorable innings.

Steve's batting technique was a reflection of his determination to succeed. He practiced relentlessly, fine-tuning every aspect of his game. He would spend hours in the nets, facing bowlers of all kinds, honing his footwork, and developing an unbreakable focus. It was this dedication to his craft that set him apart from his peers.

One of the defining features of Steve Smith's batting was his incredible ability to read the game. He had an almost intuitive understanding of the bowler's intentions and field placements. This allowed him to adapt his game plan on the fly, making him a formidable opponent in any situation. He wasn't just a batsman; he was a strategist.

As his technique and mental fortitude grew, so did his run-scoring ability. Steve's Test match performances were nothing short of astonishing. He played crucial innings against some of the world's best bowling attacks, often rescuing Australia from difficult situations. His ability to absorb pressure and steer the team to safety earned him the nickname "Captain Courageous."

One of the most iconic moments in Steve Smith's career came during the 2013-14 Ashes series. Facing England's relentless pace attack, he scored a magnificent 111 in the first Test at the Gabba. This century marked his arrival on the international stage as a force to be reckoned with. Australia went on to win the series 5-0, and Steve Smith's contributions were instrumental in the victory.

Smith's appetite for runs was insatiable. He consistently piled on the runs in Test matches and earned a reputation as one of the world's best Test batsmen. His ability to wear down bowlers with his unyielding concentration and ability to accumulate runs made him a nightmare for opposing teams.

Steve Smith

In addition to Test cricket, Steve Smith also excelled in the limited-overs formats. He played crucial roles in One Day Internationals (ODIs) and T20 matches, showcasing his adaptability and versatility as a batsman. Whether it was playing anchor in ODIs or launching big shots in T20s, Smith's batting was a sight to behold.

However, greatness often comes with its share of challenges, and Steve Smith's career was no exception. In the next chapter, we will explore one of the most significant challenges he faced—the ball-tampering scandal—and how he managed to overcome it on his path to redemption.

Chapter 5: The Captaincy Challenge

Steve Smith's tenure as the captain of the Australian cricket team reached its defining moment on a fateful day in March 2018 during the third Test match against South Africa in Cape Town. This chapter delves into the infamous Sandpaper Scandal, a pivotal and controversial chapter in Smith's career.

The series against South Africa was already a tense affair, marked by on-field clashes and heightened emotions. As Australia batted in the third Test, events took a shocking turn. Cameron Bancroft, a young opener in the team, was caught on camera using sandpaper to tamper with the ball, an act that goes against the spirit of cricket.

The images of Bancroft's actions spread like wildfire, causing a media frenzy and a worldwide outcry. The Australian team was accused of cheating, and Steve Smith, as the captain, found himself at the centre of the storm. It was a moment that would forever alter the course of his career.

Smith, along with Vice-Captain David Warner and Bancroft, faced severe consequences. All three players were handed significant suspensions by Cricket Australia. Smith and Warner were banned from international and domestic cricket for one year, while Bancroft received a nine-month suspension. Their reputations were tarnished, and the cricketing world was left in shock.

Steve Smith

Smith, in a press conference following the incident, took full responsibility for the scandal. He admitted that he had failed as a leader and let down not only his team but also the cricketing community. His actions were met with a mix of disappointment, sympathy, and anger from cricket fans and pundits alike.

The fallout from the Sandpaper Scandal extended beyond suspensions. Steve Smith was stripped of his captaincy, and Tim Paine took over as the leader of the Australian cricket team. Smith's dreams of captaining his country, a dream he had cherished since childhood, had been shattered.

During the period of suspension, Steve Smith underwent a period of deep introspection. He used the time to reflect on his actions, the values of the game, and what it truly meant to be a leader. He also focused on his physical and mental fitness, determined to return to international cricket stronger than ever.

Smith's journey to redemption was a testament to his resilience and determination. He made amends by speaking at schools and cricket clubs about the importance of fair play and the consequences of poor choices. He worked tirelessly on rebuilding his reputation and regaining the trust of fans.

The end of his suspension period marked a new beginning for Steve Smith. He returned to international cricket with a renewed sense of purpose and a determination to let his bat do the talking. His performances on the field showcased his unwavering commitment to the game and his team.

Steve Smith

In the chapters that follow, we will explore Steve Smith's remarkable comeback, his continued contributions to Australian cricket, and the lessons he learned from the Sandpaper Scandal—a chapter in his life that tested his character and ultimately helped shape his future endeavours on and off the field.

Chapter 6: The Ashes Battles

Steve Smith's journey through the ups and downs of cricket continued, marked by some of the most iconic moments in the sport's history. This chapter focuses on his unforgettable performances in the Ashes series and his pivotal role in the intense battles against England.

The Ashes, the historic rivalry between England and Australia, is the pinnacle of Test cricket. It's a series that has been steeped in tradition and drama for over a century. Steve Smith's impact on this storied rivalry is nothing short of legendary.

In the 2013-14 Ashes series, Smith played a crucial role in Australia's 5-0 whitewash of

England. His century in the first Test at the Gabba set the tone for the series, and he continued to pile on the runs, tormenting England's bowlers with his unorthodox but highly effective technique.

However, it was during the 2017-18 Ashes series in Australia that Steve Smith's true genius as a batsman came to the fore. He was the captain and the linchpin of the Australian batting order, and he delivered in spectacular fashion. Smith scored an incredible 687 runs in just seven innings, including three centuries. His ability to navigate England's seam and swing bowling, even under challenging conditions, was a masterclass in itself.

One particular innings during that series stands out—a magnificent 239 at the WACA in Perth. Smith's marathon knock not only helped

Australia win the Test but also ensured the Ashes would return Down Under. His performance earned him accolades from cricketing greats and cemented his status as one of the finest Test batsmen of his era.

Smith's battles with England's bowlers, especially their spearhead James Anderson, added an extra layer of drama to the Ashes contests. The duels between Smith's unorthodox technique and Anderson's precision were a sight to behold, captivating cricket fans around the world.

In the 2019 Ashes series in England, Steve Smith faced a challenge of a different kind. Having returned to international cricket after the Sandpaper Scandal, he was determined to prove himself once again. And he did just that. Smith was the standout performer in the series,

Steve Smith

scoring an astonishing 774 runs in just seven innings, despite missing one Test due to a concussion.

However, it wasn't just Smith's batting that left a lasting impression. His willingness to stand up to England's hostile crowd, who often taunted him with sandpaper-related chants, showed his mental resilience. Smith's determination to overcome adversity and continue to score runs for his team was a testament to his character.

Steve Smith's Ashes battles were more than just cricket matches; they were a showcase of his unwavering commitment to the Baggy Green and his ability to rise to the occasion when it mattered most. His performances in these iconic series cemented his legacy as one of Australia's greatest Test cricketers and one of the most

Steve Smith

enigmatic figures in the history of the Ashes rivalry.

Chapter 7: The Unconventional Genius

Steve Smith's cricketing journey is not only marked by his exceptional talent but also by his unique and often unconventional batting habits and quirks. This chapter explores the idiosyncrasies that define his batting style and set him apart as a truly exceptional cricketer.

From the early days of his cricketing career, it was clear that Steve Smith was no ordinary batsman. His batting technique, characterized by an unorthodox shuffle across the crease, raised eyebrows and questions. Yet, it was precisely these quirks that would make him one of the most distinctive and successful batsmen in the world.

At the heart of Smith's batting technique was his distinctive footwork. Instead of the traditional stillness at the crease, he employed a unique shuffle, moving his front foot well across to the off-side, almost outside the line of the leg stump. It was a stance that defied convention, but it worked wonders for him.

Smith's unorthodox technique served several purposes. It allowed him to play the ball late, read the bowler's line and length with precision, and adjust his shots accordingly. His shuffle also helped him in combating swing and seam movement, making him a formidable opponent in challenging conditions.

One of the most fascinating aspects of Smith's batting was his uncanny ability to pick gaps in the field. He seemed to have an innate understanding of where the fielders were placed, and he would consistently thread the ball through the smallest of openings. His unconventional footwork played a crucial role in his ability to manipulate the field.

Smith's unique style extended to his shot selection. He had a wide range of unorthodox shots in his repertoire, from the paddle sweep to the switch-hit. These shots allowed him to disrupt the bowler's line and length and keep the fielding side constantly guessing. They became a hallmark of his batting.

Perhaps the most remarkable trait of Smith's batting was his unbreakable concentration. He could bat for hours on end, seemingly impervious to fatigue or distraction. His unorthodox technique, combined with his intense focus, made him a batsman who could grind down the opposition and demoralize bowlers.

However, Smith's quirks weren't limited to his batting technique alone. He had a set of unique rituals and routines that he followed religiously before and during his innings. From touching his shoelaces to fidgeting with his helmet, these quirks became part of the Steve Smith legend.

Smith's batting habits and quirks were a reflection of his meticulous approach to the game. He was a cricketer who valued preparation and routine, and these eccentricities were an integral part of his mental preparation.

In the chapters that follow, we will delve deeper into Steve Smith's career, exploring his record-breaking achievements, his leadership on the field, and the impact he had on Australian cricket. His journey as an unconventional genius continues to inspire cricketers and cricket enthusiasts around the world.

Chapter 8: The Record-Breaking Achievements

Steve Smith's cricketing career is a symphony of records and achievements that have left an indelible mark on the sport. This chapter delves into the milestones and records that stand as a testament to his unparalleled excellence as a batsman.

From his earliest days in the Australian cricket team, it was evident that Steve Smith possessed the potential to achieve greatness. As he honed his craft, he began breaking records and setting new benchmarks, carving a place for himself in the annals of cricket history.

Steve Smith

One of Smith's most remarkable records is his consistent run-scoring in Test cricket. He achieved the fastest ever Test century by an Australian, reaching the milestone in just 69 balls against England in 2013. This record-breaking century showcased his ability to dominate opposition bowling attacks with both speed and precision.

In the 2014-15 Border-Gavaskar Trophy series against India, Smith's incredible form saw him score four centuries in four consecutive Tests, a feat previously accomplished only by the cricketing legends Don Bradman and Jacques Kallis. This remarkable consistency earned him the nickname "Captain Courageous" and solidified his status as one of the world's best Test batsmen.

Steve Smith

Smith's extraordinary run-scoring extended to his performances against England in Ashes series. During the 2015 Ashes series in England, he became the youngest Australian captain to score an Ashes double century. His 215 at Lord's was a masterclass in patience and resilience, cementing his reputation as a modern-day batting maestro.

In 2017, Smith achieved the highest batting ranking points ever recorded by an Australian Test batsman, surpassing the legendary Sir Don Bradman. This remarkable achievement underscored his dominance in the format and his ability to consistently outperform his peers.

Smith's record-breaking streak also extended to the limited-overs formats. In One Day Internationals (ODIs), he became the fastest Australian to reach 3,000, 4,000, and 5,000 runs. His remarkable performances in ODIs solidified his reputation as a complete batsman capable of excelling in all formats of the game.

In Twenty20 Internationals (T20Is), Smith's ability to adapt his game to the shortest format of cricket was evident. He achieved the record for the highest individual score by an Australian in a T20I, scoring an unbeaten 90 runs against England in 2018.Steve Smith's record-breaking achievements are not just a testament to his individual brilliance but also a reflection of his unwavering dedication to the game. Each record and milestone is a chapter in the story of a cricketer who has redefined the art of batting with his unique style and insatiable hunger for runs.

In the chapters that follow, we will explore more facets of Steve Smith's career, his leadership on the field, and the impact he has had on Australian cricket as a whole. His journey is not just a story of records; it's a narrative of excellence that continues to inspire cricketers and cricket enthusiasts around the world.

Chapter 9: Off the Field

While Steve Smith's cricketing prowess has earned him accolades and records on the field, this chapter offers a glimpse into the facets of his life outside of cricket. It paints a portrait of the man beyond the boundary, his interests, hobbies, and his contributions to society.

Steve Smith's life away from the cricket pitch is a captivating blend of various passions and pursuits. One of the most notable aspects of his life off the field is his deep love for music. When he's not facing bowlers on the pitch, he often finds solace in strumming his guitar. Music serves as both a creative outlet and a source of relaxation for the cricketing maestro.

Steve Smith

Another facet of Steve's life revolves around his passion for travel. His cricketing career has taken him to destinations around the world, and he relishes the opportunity to explore diverse cultures and cuisines. These experiences have broadened his horizons and enriched his perspective on life.

Beyond personal interests, Steve Smith is dedicated to making a positive impact on society. He engages in charitable activities and actively supports various causes. His involvement in initiatives aimed at helping underprivileged children and promoting animal welfare exemplifies his compassionate side.Steve often visits schools and interacts with young cricket enthusiasts, imparting wisdom and inspiration to the next generation of cricketers. He understands the significance of nurturing talent at the grassroots level and is passionate about promoting the sport he loves.

Family remains an integral part of Steve's life. He shares a close bond with his parents, Peter and Gillian, who have been steadfast supporters of his cricketing journey since its inception. Their presence at his matches and their unwavering encouragement have been a constant source of strength.

Steve's personal life also includes his wife, Dani Willis, whom he married in 2018. Their relationship is a testament to the importance of a strong support system for athletes who lead demanding professional lives. Dani has been a pillar of strength, providing unwavering support during the highs and lows of Steve's career.

These glimpses into Steve Smith's life off the field reveal a well-rounded individual who values balance, creativity, and compassion. While he may be celebrated as a cricketing icon, it is his multifaceted personality and his commitment to making a positive impact that further solidify his status as a role model both within and beyond the cricketing fraternity.

Smith breaks down during the Sandpaper press
conference

Smith has shown he can perform on all the cricketing world stages

Steve Smith

Smith has proven himself a brilliant white ball batsman

Steve Smith

Smith celebrates another Test hundred

Chapter 10: Facing Adversity

Life in the world of professional cricket is not always a smooth sail, and Steve Smith's journey has been no exception. This chapter delves into the adversities he faced, both on and off the field, and the remarkable resilience that defined his response to these challenges.

The Sandpaper Scandal in South Africa in 2018 stands as one of the most significant adversities in Steve Smith's career. As the captain of the Australian cricket team, he was embroiled in a controversy that shook the cricketing world. The scandal resulted in his suspension, the loss of his captaincy, and severe damage to his reputation.

Steve Smith

In the face of immense public scrutiny and criticism, Steve Smith demonstrated exceptional resilience. He acknowledged his mistakes, accepted responsibility, and embarked on a journey of redemption. He used the suspension period to reflect on his actions, seek guidance, and work on both his physical and mental fitness.

Smith's return to international cricket post-suspension was met with intense scrutiny and pressure. The adversities he faced extended to the hostile crowds and taunts from opposing fans, often referencing the Sandpaper Scandal. However, he remained steadfast, displaying remarkable mental fortitude in the face of adversity.

In August 2019, during the Ashes series in England, Smith faced a different kind of adversity. He suffered a concussion after being struck on the head by a Jofra Archer bouncer. Despite the physical and mental challenges that followed, Smith made a triumphant return to the series, highlighting his resilience and commitment to the game.

Chapter 11: Leading by Example

Steve Smith's captaincy of the Australian cricket team was marked by a unique blend of leadership, determination, and setting the highest standards. This chapter delves into his time as captain and the impact he had on the team, both as a batsman and a leader.

When Steve Smith was appointed as the captain of the Australian cricket team in 2015, he embraced the role with a sense of purpose and a vision for the future. His leadership style was characterized by leading from the front, setting an example through his performances, and demanding excellence from his teammates.

Steve Smith

As captain, Smith faced the challenging task of rebuilding the team after the retirements of stalwarts like Ricky Ponting and Michael Clarke. He nurtured young talent, provided opportunities to promising players, and fostered a sense of camaraderie within the squad. His ability to inspire and lead by example was evident in the team's improved performances.

One of the defining moments of Smith's captaincy was the 2017-18 Ashes series in Australia. Facing England, he led the team to a resounding 4-0 series victory. Smith's performances with the bat were exceptional, scoring an astonishing 687 runs in just seven innings. His leadership during that series played a pivotal role in the team's success.

Smith's leadership extended beyond the cricket field. He understood the importance of being a spokesperson for the game and worked tirelessly to promote cricket at the grassroots level. He engaged with fans, interacted with aspiring cricketers, and actively contributed to the growth of the sport.

One of the challenges Smith faced during his captaincy was the fallout from the Sandpaper Scandal in South Africa. He accepted responsibility for the incident and faced severe consequences, including suspension and the loss of captaincy. However, his actions during the period of suspension and his commitment to redemption showcased his resilience and leadership qualities.

Smith's return to international cricket after the suspension was a defining moment in his career. Despite the adversities and scrutiny, he continued to lead by example with his performances. His leadership on the field and his determination to make amends set a standard for perseverance and resilience.

Chapter 12: The Global T20 Circuit

Steve Smith's cricketing journey is not confined to international matches alone. This chapter takes you into the exciting world of T20 leagues around the globe where Smith has showcased his skills, adapting to the shortest format of the game with flair and versatility.T20 cricket, with its fast-paced nature and dynamic gameplay, has become a prominent fixture in the international cricket calendar. Steve Smith, known for his classical Test batting, has proven his adaptability by excelling in the high-octane world of T20s.Smith's global T20 odyssey began with the Indian Premier League (IPL), one of the most prestigious and high-profile T20 leagues in the world. He was picked up by the Rajasthan

Steve Smith

Royals in the inaugural season in 2008. Over the years, he established himself as a key player for the franchise, showcasing his ability to anchor the innings or accelerate as required.

In 2017, Smith's exceptional performances in the IPL earned him the captaincy of the Rising Pune Supergiant, where he led the team to the final. His leadership and batting prowess made him a sought-after commodity in the league.

The IPL was just the beginning of Smith's global T20 journey. He has plied his trade in various T20 leagues across the world, including the Big Bash League (BBL) in Australia and the Caribbean Premier League (CPL). His adaptability to different conditions and his ability to perform consistently in T20 cricket have made him a valuable asset for franchise teams.

Steve Smith

Smith's overseas stints in T20 leagues have not only allowed him to fine-tune his skills in the format but also exposed him to diverse cricketing cultures. He has shared dressing rooms with some of the world's best T20 players, gaining insights and experiences that have enhanced his overall cricketing repertoire.

One of the highlights of Smith's T20 career came in 2020 when he was appointed captain of the Rajasthan Royals for the IPL season. His leadership and batting were instrumental in guiding the team to playoff contention, demonstrating his versatility as a leader in the shortest format of the game.

Beyond the statistics and scores, Smith's contributions to various T20 franchises have solidified his reputation as a versatile cricketer who can thrive in any format. His ability to adapt, innovate, and lead in the fast-paced world of T20 cricket showcases his all-round cricketing prowess.

In the chapters that follow, we will continue to explore Steve Smith's cricketing journey, his leadership, and the impact he has had on Australian cricket. His global T20 adventures have not only expanded his horizons but have also contributed to his growth as a cricketer who can excel on any stage.

Chapter 13: A Legacy in the Making

As Steve Smith's cricketing journey continues to unfold, it becomes increasingly evident that he is in the process of crafting a legacy that will leave an indelible mark on the sport. This chapter delves into the ongoing chapters of his career and the lasting impact he is making in the world of cricket.

Smith's career trajectory has been one of remarkable highs and the ability to rebound from significant lows. His journey is a testament to his unwavering determination, unmatched work ethic, and the relentless pursuit of excellence. His ability to adapt to different formats of the game and evolve as a cricketer is a quality that sets him apart as a true cricketing genius.

In the Test arena, Smith continues to be a linchpin of the Australian batting lineup. His insatiable appetite for runs and his ability to counter opposition bowlers in all conditions are qualities that bode well for the future of Australian cricket. As a leader in the longest format, he sets the bar high not only with his performances but also with his approach to the game.

In the limited-overs formats, Smith's versatility as a batsman is more evident than ever. He can anchor an innings in One Day Internationals (ODIs) or provide explosive starts in Twenty20 Internationals (T20Is). His adaptability ensures

that he remains a vital component of the
Australian team in white-ball cricket.

Beyond his individual accomplishments, Smith's
leadership qualities continue to shine. Whether
captaining a franchise in the Indian Premier
League (IPL) or contributing as a senior player in
the national team, his leadership is marked by
setting high standards and leading by example.

Smith's impact reaches beyond the boundary
ropes. His involvement in charitable activities
and his commitment to promoting the growth
of cricket, especially at the grassroots level,
exemplify his dedication to the sport and its
future. He is not just a cricketer but also an
ambassador for the game.

As Steve Smith's career unfolds, the chapters yet
to be written hold the promise of further
records, milestones, and moments of brilliance.

His journey is a testament to the enduring spirit of a cricketer who has overcome adversity, triumphed on the world stage, and continues to inspire the next generation of cricketers.

In concluding this book, it's clear that Steve Smith's legacy is not just in the making; it's already an integral part of the rich tapestry of cricketing history. His story is one of resilience, adaptability, and an unyielding commitment to the sport he loves. As his career continues to evolve, his legacy will only grow, leaving an enduring impact on the world of cricket for generations to come.

Chapter 14: Steve Smith's Charitable Endeavours

Beyond the cricket field, Steve Smith has shown his commitment to making a positive impact on society through his involvement in charitable activities. This chapter sheds light on his philanthropic efforts and the causes he supports.

Steve Smith's dedication to giving back to the community is evident in his active engagement with various charitable organizations and initiatives. He understands the platform that his cricketing success provides and uses it as an opportunity to make a difference in the lives of others.

One of the causes close to Steve's heart is the well-being of underprivileged children. He has been actively involved in initiatives aimed at providing educational opportunities and support to children in need. His visits to schools, interactions with young cricket enthusiasts, and inspirational talks serve as a source of motivation for the next generation.

Smith's passion for animal welfare is another facet of his charitable work. He has actively supported organizations and campaigns that focus on the welfare and conservation of wildlife. His love for animals extends to his own pet dogs, and he has used his platform to raise awareness about responsible pet ownership.

Steve Smith

In times of crisis, Smith has not hesitated to lend a helping hand. He has been part of fundraising efforts to support disaster relief, whether it be for bushfire victims in Australia or other humanitarian causes around the world. His willingness to use his influence to mobilize support for those in need showcases his compassionate nature.

Through his involvement in charitable events and campaigns, Smith has inspired others to join in making a positive impact. His active participation in charity matches and events has not only raised funds but also increased awareness about various social and environmental issues.

Smith's wife, Dani Willis, has been a supportive partner in his charitable endeavours, often joining him in these initiatives. Together, they have worked to create a positive influence and encourage others to contribute to meaningful causes.

While Steve Smith's cricketing exploits have made him a sports icon, it is his commitment to making a difference beyond the boundary that defines him as a compassionate individual and a responsible global citizen. His philanthropic efforts serve as an inspiration to athletes and fans alike, showcasing the power of sports to effect positive change in the world.

Bonus: Fascinating Facts About Cricket

Cricket, often dubbed "the gentleman's game," is filled with rich history, intriguing traditions, and captivating anecdotes. This chapter takes you on a journey through some of the most fascinating and lesser-known facts about the sport of cricket.

Oldest Cricket Club: The Marylebone Cricket Club (MCC), founded in 1787, is one of the world's oldest cricket clubs. They are responsible for drafting the original laws of cricket, which still form the basis of the game today.

Steve Smith

Longest Test Match: The longest Test match in cricket history took place between South Africa and England in 1939. It stretched over 14 days, with eight days lost to rain, making it the longest cricket match ever recorded.

Only Batsman to Score 400 in an Innings: In 2004, Brian Lara of the West Indies became the first and only batsman to score 400 runs in a single Test innings against England.

Cricket and Politics: Cricket and politics often intersect. During the apartheid era, South Africa was banned from international cricket, and cricket played a significant role in the anti-apartheid movement.

The Ashes Urn: The Ashes urn, a symbol of the legendary England vs. Australia rivalry, is believed to contain the ashes of a burnt cricket bail. It was presented to England captain Ivo

Bligh after England's victory in 1882-83, and the tradition of the Ashes series was born.

W.G. Grace's Beard: W.G. Grace, one of cricket's early legends, had such a long and bushy beard that he tucked it into his belt when batting.

Cricket in Space: In 2014, an astronaut aboard the International Space Station played cricket in zero gravity, proving that cricket truly knows no boundaries.

Bizarre Dismissals: Cricket has witnessed some strange dismissals, including being hit by a flying seagull, a ball getting stuck in a helmet, and even a batsman being given out "obstructing the field."

The Mystery of Ball Tampering: Ball tampering, a controversial aspect of the game, involves altering the condition of the cricket ball to gain an advantage. This has led to suspensions, bans, and heated debates.

Lords' Cricket Ground: Known as the "Home of Cricket," Lords' Cricket Ground in London has a slope across the pitch. It's one of the few cricket grounds with this unique feature, which impacts the ball's movement.

Unbreakable Record: In 1956, Jim Laker took 19 wickets in a single Test match for England against Australia, a record that still stands.

Cricket Diplomacy: India and Pakistan have often used cricket as a means of diplomacy. Matches between the two nations, known as "cricket diplomacy," have played a role in improving relations.

Duckworth-Lewis Method: The Duckworth-Lewis method, used in rain-affected limited-overs matches, was invented by two statisticians, Frank Duckworth and Tony Lewis, to determine revised targets. It's now a standard part of the game.

Most Run-Outs in a Ball: In a peculiar incident, three batsmen were run out off a single delivery during a domestic game in South Africa. It's one of the rarest occurrences in cricket history.

These fascinating facts only scratch the surface of the rich tapestry of cricket. The sport continues to evolve, amaze, and captivate fans worldwide with its traditions, records, and the endless stories it generates on and off the field.

adapt to different situations, and remain calm in challenging circumstances set him apart as a leader who led from the front.

Glossary:

Test Cricket: The longest format of international cricket, usually played over five days, known for its emphasis on skill and endurance.

ODI (One Day International): A limited-overs format of cricket where each team is allowed a maximum of 50 overs to bat and bowl.T20 (Twenty20): The shortest format of cricket, with each team facing a maximum of 20 overs per innings, known for its fast-paced and entertaining nature.

Century: When a batsman scores 100 runs in a single innings.

Steve Smith

Captaincy: The role of leading and making strategic decisions for a cricket team, often held by a senior and influential player.

Sandpaper Scandal: The controversial incident in which Steve Smith and other Australian cricketers were involved in ball tampering during a Test match in South Africa in 2018.Resilience: The ability to bounce back from setbacks, challenges, or adversities.

Redemption: The act of making amends for past mistakes or wrongdoings.

IPL (Indian Premier League): A popular T20 cricket league in India, featuring teams from various cities and attracting international stars.

Adversity: Difficulties, setbacks, or unfavourable circumstances that one may face in cricket or life.

Steve Smith

Legacy: The lasting impact, influence, or reputation that a cricketer like Steve Smith leaves behind in the sport.

Global T20 Circuit: The network of various T20 cricket leagues played worldwide, where players like Steve Smith participate in addition to international matches.

Duckworth-Lewis Method: A mathematical formula used to adjust targets in rain-affected limited-overs matches, ensuring fairness.

Cricket Diplomacy: The use of cricket matches between countries, such as India and Pakistan, as a means to improve political relations.

Gentleman's Game: A term often used to describe cricket due to its historical association with sportsmanship and fair play.